Instant Cartoons
for Church Newsletters

George W. Knight *Compiler*

BAKER BOOK HOUSE
Grand Rapids, Michigan 49516

Introduction

Thousands of copies of the previous five books in this series—Instant Cartoons 1, 2, 3, 4, and 5—have been sold. This proves there is a need for cartoons with a Christian slant designed for publication in local church newsletters and worship bulletins.

In *Instant Cartoons #6* you will find the same wholesome humor and high-quality cartoon drawings that you have come to appreciate in the other books in this series. Included are more than one hundred cartoons that have been created by three cartoonists to give you a variety of styles and approaches. Each cartoon is published in two sizes as a convenience to church newsletter editors. All you do is clip and publish the size that fits the space you have available in your newsletter or worship bulletin.

It would help me in planning future books of these Instant Cartoons if I knew how you are using this material in your local church publications. Write me and include two or three issues of your newsletter or bulletin in which these cartoons appear. The address is Baker Book House, P. O. Box 6287, Grand Rapids, MI 49516.

George W. Knight

About the cartoonists . . .

Jack Hamm is a Christian artist from Dallas, Texas. For more than thirty-five years he has shared his faith through his religious drawings. His work has appeared in scores of daily and weekly newspapers and national Christian publications.

Goddard Sherman is a retired United Methodist minister who resides in Valdosta, Georgia. His cartoons have appeared in several national magazines as well as numerous church publications.

Joe McKeever is pastor of the First Baptist Church of Kenner, Louisiana. A member of the National Cartoonist's Society, he creates cartoons that appear regularly in Southern Baptist newspapers as well as several general religious publications.

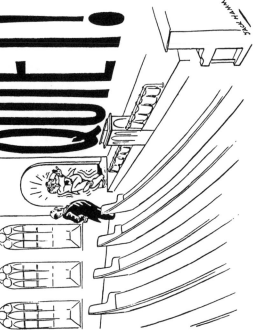

"I HAD IT PAINTED TO STOP ALL THIS CHIT-CHAT BEFORE THE SERVICE."

"SOMETIMES HUBERT GETS THE NOTION THAT REV. RIPPLE IS REFERRING TO HIM IN HIS SIN SERMONS."

"A 'SAINT' BERNARD YOU SAY . . . PAYING AN ECCLESIASTICAL CALL, NO DOUBT . . . PLEASE SHOW HIM IN, GRISWOLD."

"I LOVE TO HEAR YOU PREACH. YOU GET SO MANY THINGS OUT OF YOUR TEXT THAT ARE REALLY NOT THERE."

"SOMETIMES HUBERT GETS THE NOTION THAT REV. RIPPLE IS REFERRING TO HIM IN HIS SIN SERMONS."

"I HAD IT PAINTED TO STOP ALL THIS CHIT-CHAT BEFORE THE SERVICE."

"I LOVE TO HEAR YOU PREACH. YOU GET SO MANY THINGS OUT OF YOUR TEXT THAT ARE REALLY NOT THERE."

"A 'SAINT' BERNARD YOU SAY . . . PAYING AN ECCLESIASTICAL CALL, NO DOUBT . . . PLEASE SHOW HIM IN, GRISWOLD."

"YUP, PARSON, MY MAMA SAYS A PRAYER FOR ME EVERY NIGHT. SHE SAYS, "THANK HEAVEN YOU'RE IN BED!""

"'SILVER AND GOLD HAVE I NONE,' DECLARED SIMON PETER TO THE LAME MAN AT THE GATE OF THE TEMPLE. WHAT FURTHER PROOF IS NEEDED THAT PETER WAS A PREACHER?"

"MY MAMA IS WEARING A NEW SPRING OUTFIT AND MY FATHER SAID HE'D BE AT THE MOURNER'S BENCH."

"WELL, I KNOW MY DADDY IS SMARTER THAN YOURS 'CAUSE HE'S A BIG DEMON IN THE CHURCH!"

"'SILVER AND GOLD HAVE I NONE,'
DECLARED SIMON PETER TO THE LAME
MAN AT THE GATE OF THE TEMPLE. WHAT
FURTHER PROOF IS NEEDED THAT PETER
WAS A PREACHER?"

"YUP, PARSON, MY MAMA SAYS A PRAYER
FOR ME EVERY NIGHT. SHE SAYS, 'THANK
HEAVEN YOU'RE IN BED!'"

"MY MAMA IS WEARING A NEW SPRING
OUTFIT AND MY FATHER SAID HE'D BE AT
THE MOURNER'S BENCH."

"WELL, I KNOW MY DADDY IS SMARTER
THAN YOURS 'CAUSE HE'S A BIG DEMON
IN THE CHURCH!"

"WHEN YOU SAY, 'WHO'LL BE THE FIRST TO RISE, THEREBY INDICATING A PLEDGE OF $5,000,' ALL YOU HAVE TO DO IS THROW SWITCH 'A,' WHICH CONNECTS TO SEAT 'B.'"

"THE REVEREND DR. JOSHKINS WILL LECTURE ON 'FOOLS' IN THE CENTRAL AVENUE CHURCH MONDAY EVENING, AND I TRUST A GREAT MANY WILL ATTEND."

"OFF THE CUFF LET ME SAY THE SWAB IS PAYING ME EXACTLY NOTHING AS HIS PULPIT SUPPLY."

"THE REVEREND DR. JOSHKINS WILL LECTURE ON 'FOOLS' IN THE CENTRAL AVENUE CHURCH MONDAY EVENING, AND I TRUST A GREAT MANY WILL ATTEND."

"WHEN YOU SAY, 'WHO'LL BE THE FIRST TO RISE, THEREBY INDICATING A PLEDGE OF $5,000,' ALL YOU HAVE TO DO IS THROW SWITCH 'A,' WHICH CONNECTS TO SEAT 'B.'"

AJAX VAN LINES

DURING THE PAST FEW WEEKS WE HAVE MOVED 60 CLERGYMEN TO THE ENTIRE SATISFACTION OF ALL CONCERNED

"OFF THE CUFF LET ME SAY THE SWAB IS PAYING ME EXACTLY NOTHING AS HIS PULPIT SUPPLY."

"AFTER ALL, MINE IS NEW, AND I'M PROUD OF IT TOO."

"WOULD THOSE WHO ARE IN THE HABIT OF PUTTING BUTTONS IN THE COLLECTION PLATE KINDLY USE THEIR OWN BUTTONS AND NOT THOSE ON THE PEW CUSHIONS."

"REGARDING THE REFRESHMENTS FOR THE CHURCH SOCIAL, LADIES, WHAT WE WANT ARE NOT ABSTRACT PROMISES BUT CONCRETE CAKE."

"NOT SO REVERENT, BUT IT SURE REGAINS THEIR ATTENTION!"

"WOULD THOSE WHO ARE IN THE HABIT OF PUTTING BUTTONS IN THE COLLECTION PLATE KINDLY USE THEIR OWN BUTTONS AND NOT THOSE ON THE PEW CUSHIONS."

"AFTER ALL, MINE IS NEW, AND I'M PROUD OF IT TOO."

"NOT SO REVERENT, BUT IT SURE REGAINS THEIR ATTENTION!"

"REGARDING THE REFRESHMENTS FOR THE CHURCH SOCIAL, LADIES, WHAT WE WANT ARE NOT ABSTRACT PROMISES BUT CONCRETE CAKE."

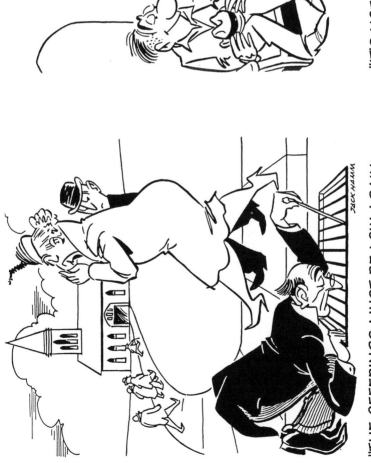

"THE OFFERINGS MUST BE LOW AGAIN . . . THERE GOES REV. RIPPLE WITH HIS GUM-ON-A-STICK ROUTINE."

"IT'S NOT THE SPIRIT OF THE GIFT I WISH TO QUESTION, IT'S . . . WELL, REGARDING YOUR BUSINESS OF COUNTERFEITING . . . "

"IN FACT, AS A YOUNG COUNTRY PREACHER I ATE SO MUCH OF IT FRIED, FOR A WHILE I THOUGHT I MIGHT TURN INTO ONE."

"THE DOG? DON'T WORRY ABOUT HIM, PARSON. . . . HE ONLY BITES SCOUNDRELS."

"THE OFFERINGS MUST BE LOW AGAIN . . .
THERE GOES REV. RIPPLE WITH HIS GUM-
ON-A-STICK ROUTINE."

"IT'S NOT THE SPIRIT OF THE GIFT I WISH TO
QUESTION, IT'S . . . WELL, REGARDING
YOUR BUSINESS OF COUNTERFEITING . . . "

"THE DOG? DON'T WORRY ABOUT HIM,
PARSON. . . . HE ONLY BITES
SCOUNDRELS."

"IN FACT, AS A YOUNG COUNTRY
PREACHER I ATE SO MUCH OF IT FRIED,
FOR A WHILE I THOUGHT I MIGHT TURN
INTO ONE."

"REMEMBER OUR DEAL, HARRIGAN—WE SPLIT THE RICE AFTER THIS EVENING'S WEDDING."

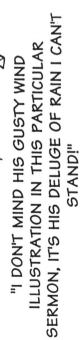

"I DON'T MIND HIS GUSTY WIND ILLUSTRATION IN THIS PARTICULAR SERMON, IT'S HIS DELUGE OF RAIN I CAN'T STAND!"

"THE COTTON? OH, HE NEVER LIKES TO
HEAR HIS SERMONS A SECOND TIME."

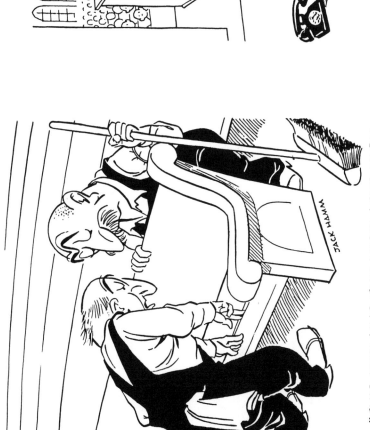

"THIS EXPLAINS THE MISPLACED HIGH
NOTE WE HEARD LAST SUNDAY . . . THESE
TWO BOARDS PINCH WHERE THEY COME
TOGETHER."

"I DON'T MIND HIS GUSTY WIND ILLUSTRATION IN THIS PARTICULAR SERMON, IT'S HIS DELUGE OF RAIN I CAN'T STAND!"

"REMEMBER OUR DEAL, HARRIGAN—WE SPLIT THE RICE AFTER THIS EVENING'S WEDDING."

"THIS EXPLAINS THE MISPLACED HIGH NOTE WE HEARD LAST SUNDAY . . . THESE TWO BOARDS PINCH WHERE THEY COME TOGETHER."

"THE COTTON? OH, HE NEVER LIKES TO HEAR HIS SERMONS A SECOND TIME."

"WHILE I THINK OF IT, JENKINS, PLEASE TIGHTEN THE LIGHT BULBS OVER THE CHOIR LOFT."

"AS THE BACK ROW FILLS UP PASTOR PEAK PUSHES A BUTTON THAT MOVES IT TO THE FRONT."

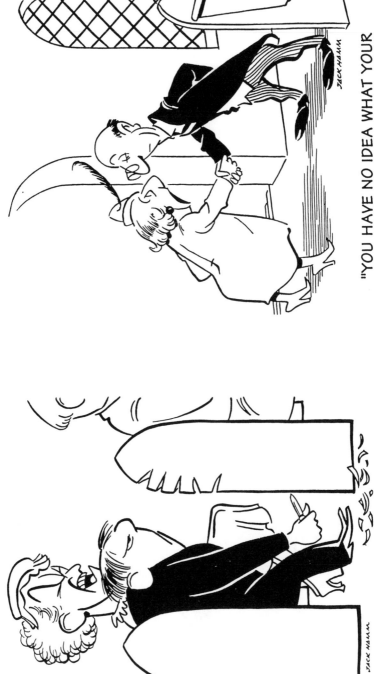

"YOU HAVE NO IDEA WHAT YOUR SERMONS MEAN TO MY HUSBAND SINCE HE'S LOST HIS MIND."

"OH, STOP CARVING A NOTCH EVERY TIME HE SAYS 'IN CONCLUSION'!"

"AS THE BACK ROW FILLS UP PASTOR PEAK PUSHES A BUTTON THAT MOVES IT TO THE FRONT."

"WHILE I THINK OF IT, JENKINS, PLEASE TIGHTEN THE LIGHT BULBS OVER THE CHOIR LOFT."

"OH, STOP CARVING A NOTCH EVERY TIME HE SAYS 'IN CONCLUSION'!"

"YOU HAVE NO IDEA WHAT YOUR SERMONS MEAN TO MY HUSBAND SINCE HE'S LOST HIS MIND."

"HE WAS A STRANGER AND I TOOK HIM IN."

FOR THE THIRD SUCCESSFUL YEAR IN A ROW, "LOOIE THE PICK POCKET" WAS IN CHARGE OF OUR FUND-RAISING CAMPAIGN."

"I HEARD THAT SAME SERMON YESTERDAY ON DIAL-A-PRAYER."

"NO, JIMMY, WE DON'T REFER TO THE DISCIPLES AS PR MEN."

"FOR THE THIRD SUCCESSFUL YEAR IN A ROW, 'LOOIE THE PICK POCKET' WAS IN CHARGE OF OUR FUND-RAISING CAMPAIGN."

"HE WAS A STRANGER AND I TOOK HIM IN."

"NO, JIMMY, WE DON'T REFER TO THE DISCIPLES AS PR MEN."

"I HEARD THAT SAME SERMON YESTERDAY ON DIAL-A-PRAYER."

"I KNOW IT'S A PRAYING MANTIS, BUT YOU CANNOT TAKE IT TO CHURCH."

"IF I BECOME 'BORN AGAIN,' CAN I FUDGE A BIT ON MY AGE?"

"MAYBE THEY'LL CONCENTRATE ON MY SERMON IF I APPEAR TO BE ON TV."

"NOT TO WORRY . . . HE'S SENDING US DOWN SOME FAST FOOD."

"IF I BECOME 'BORN AGAIN,' CAN I FUDGE A BIT ON MY AGE?"

"I KNOW IT'S A PRAYING MANTIS, BUT YOU CANNOT TAKE IT TO CHURCH."

"NOT TO WORRY . . . HE'S SENDING US DOWN SOME FAST FOOD."

"MAYBE THEY'LL CONCENTRATE ON MY SERMON IF I APPEAR TO BE ON TV."

"A PERFECT MATCH. SHE'S A HYPOCHONDRIAC AND HE'S A PILL."

"IF I GUESS WHO THE HORRIBLE EXAMPLE WAS IN YOUR SERMON, WILL YOU TELL ME?"

"ON WEDNESDAY EVENING THERE WILL BE A CONGREGATIONAL MEETING TO CONSIDER THE PURCHASE OF A NEW HEATING PLANT."

"I WISH THERE WAS A WAY WE COULD CONVINCE THE FLOCK TO GIVE UP ITS WOOL."

"IF I GUESS WHO THE HORRIBLE EXAMPLE WAS IN YOUR SERMON, WILL YOU TELL ME?"

"A PERFECT MATCH. SHE'S A HYPOCHONDRIAC AND HE'S A PILL."

"I WISH THERE WAS A WAY WE COULD CONVINCE THE FLOCK TO GIVE UP ITS WOOL."

"ON WEDNESDAY EVENING THERE WILL BE A CONGREGATIONAL MEETING TO CONSIDER THE PURCHASE OF A NEW HEATING PLANT."

"I SURE ENVY MY FOOT . . . IT SLEPT THROUGH HIS ENTIRE SERMON."

"OF COURSE HE DRAWS CROWDS . . . HE LIP-SYNCS BILLY GRAHAM!"

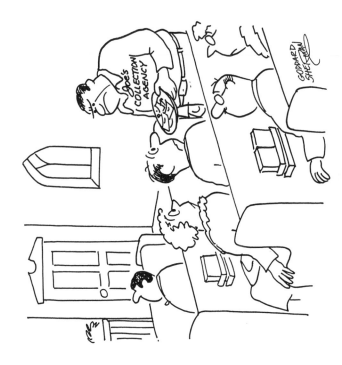

"AMEN!"

"OF COURSE HE DRAWS CROWDS . . .
HE LIP-SYNCS BILLY GRAHAM!"

"I SURE ENVY MY FOOT . . . IT SLEPT
THROUGH HIS ENTIRE SERMON."

"AMEN!"

"HE CAN'T COME NOW; HE'S PRACTICING WHAT HE PREACHES."

"CAN YOU WAIT A FEW MINUTES? MY FOLKS WANT TO FINISH THEIR FIGHT."

"YOU'RE SUPPOSED TO REPORT IT WHEN YOUR CUP RUNNETH OVER."

"I DO . . . . I DON'T . . . I DO . . . ."

"CAN YOU WAIT A FEW MINUTES?
MY FOLKS WANT TO FINISH THEIR
FIGHT."

"HE CAN'T COME NOW; HE'S
PRACTICING WHAT HE PREACHES."

"I DO . . . I DON'T . . . I DO . . ."

"YOU'RE SUPPOSED TO REPORT IT
WHEN YOUR CUP RUNNETH OVER."

"NORMALLY I'D SAY GRACE, BUT I THINK THIS CALLS FOR LAST RITES."

"IT SHOULD BE A HAPPY MARRIAGE. HE'S A GO-GETTER, AND SHE'S GOT IT."

"I'M AFRAID REPENTANCE WON'T QUITE COVER IT, REVEREND!"

"I THOUGHT YOU MIGHT LIKE TO KNOW THAT NONE OF THE SHOES IN YOUR SERMON FIT THIS MORNING."

"IT SHOULD BE A HAPPY
MARRIAGE. HE'S A GO-GETTER,
AND SHE'S GOT IT."

"NORMALLY I'D SAY GRACE, BUT I
THINK THIS CALLS FOR LAST
RITES."

"I THOUGHT YOU MIGHT LIKE TO
KNOW THAT NONE OF THE SHOES
IN YOUR SERMON FIT THIS
MORNING."

"I'M AFRAID REPENTANCE WON'T
QUITE COVER IT, REVEREND!"

"STEAK? BUT YOU SAID WE WERE HAVING A BIG TURKEY FOR DINNER!"

"WE DON'T REFER TO A BOUNTIFUL COLLECTION AS HITTING THE JACKPOT."

"FOR RICHER OR POORER? OH, I'LL TAKE RICHER!"

"I DON'T CARE IF YOU DIDN'T LIKE THE SERMON—YOU SHOULDN'T HAVE ASKED FOR YOUR MONEY BACK."

"WE DON'T REFER TO A BOUNTIFUL COLLECTION AS HITTING THE JACKPOT."

"STEAK? BUT YOU SAID WE WERE HAVING A BIG TURKEY FOR DINNER!"

"I DON'T CARE IF YOU DIDN'T LIKE THE SERMON—YOU SHOULDN'T HAVE ASKED FOR YOUR MONEY BACK."

"FOR RICHER OR POORER? OH, I'LL TAKE RICHER!"

"YOU MEAN HIS REAL NAME OR THE ONE DAD CALLS HIM?"

"WOULDN'T IT SAVE A LOT OF TIME IF I JUST PUT THIS ON TAPE?"

"SORRY, SON, I CAN'T HELP YOU WITH YOUR SCHOOLWORK. WE HAVE TO KEEP CHURCH AND STATE SEPARATE."

"I JUST LOVE MILITARY WEDDINGS—THEY'RE SO ROMANTIC."

"WOULDN'T IT SAVE A LOT OF TIME
IF I JUST PUT THIS ON TAPE?"

"YOU MEAN HIS REAL NAME OR
THE ONE DAD CALLS HIM?"

"I JUST LOVE MILITARY
WEDDINGS—THEY'RE SO
ROMANTIC."

"SORRY, SON, I CAN'T HELP YOU
WITH YOUR SCHOOLWORK. WE HAVE
TO KEEP CHURCH AND STATE
SEPARATE."

"I THOUGHT THE BEST PART OF THE SERMON WAS WHEN THE PREACHER YELLED AND DAD WOKE UP AND FELL OFF THE SEAT!"

"WAKE UP, DEAR, AND STOP MUMBLING 'I GAVE AT THE OFFICE.'"

"NO, GEORGE WASN'T SICK. HE WAS WORSHIPING THE HOUSEHOLD IDOL."

"LOVE, HONOR, AND CHERISH, EH? COULD I PICK TWO OUT OF THREE?"

"WAKE UP, DEAR, AND STOP MUMBLING 'I GAVE AT THE OFFICE.' "

"I THOUGHT THE BEST PART OF THE SERMON WAS WHEN THE PREACHER YELLED AND DAD WOKE UP AND FELL OFF THE SEAT!"

"LOVE, HONOR, AND CHERISH, EH? COULD I PICK TWO OUT OF THREE?"

"NO, GEORGE WASN'T SICK. HE WAS WORSHIPING THE HOUSEHOLD IDOL."

"I HOPE HE REMEMBERS OUR BALL GAME AFTER THE SERVICE."

"MR. JONES SAYS THEY WRITE YOUR SERMONS."

"MR. JONES SAYS THEY WRITE YOUR SERMONS."

"I HOPE HE REMEMBERS OUR BALL GAME AFTER THE SERVICE."

"YOU CAN MAKE BETTER TIME IF YOU IMAGINE SOMEONE WAITING AT THE END GIVING YOU A WELL DONE!"

"READING FROM THE TRULY INTERNATIONAL VERSION, 'AND JESUS APPEARED IN THEIR MIDST AND SAID, BONJOUR! QUE PASA?'"

"HERE'S A SHEKEL — AT LEAST GET ME AN HONORABLE MENTION IN THE BOOK OF JUDGES."

"I DON'T WANT TO BE LISTED AS THE 'SPOKESCLERGYPERSON'— SEE IF YOUR TYPEWRITER CAN SPELL PREACHER!"

"WELL, MR. PRESIDENT, OUR CHURCH JUST LOVED YOUR LETTER — IT'S SO NICE WHEN THE HIGHER POWER TAKES NOTICE OF US!"

"AND THE DEACONS TOLD ME TO TAKE A TRIP TO THE HOLY LAND. HEY — IS THIS HOLY OR WHAT?"

"THIS JOGGING TRAIL GOES RIGHT BY THAT LITTLE CHAPEL — SO YOU CAN STOP AND ASK FOR FORGIVENESS FOR TREATING YOUR BODY LIKE THIS!"

"THEY'RE REALLY GLAD TO SEE US — THEY HAVE A HUGE BUILDING DEBT!"

WELCOME PASTOR AND FAMILY

"AS 'MISS WINSTON COUNTY FOR 1987', IT IS MY PLEASURE TO SPEAK TO YOU AVERAGE PEOPLE ON THE SUBJECT OF HANDLING FAME AND FORTUNE!"

JOE McKEEVER

"NO, I THINK HIS FUNNY STORIES ARE HILARIOUS — BUT SO ARE HIS SAD ONES!"

JOE McKEEVER

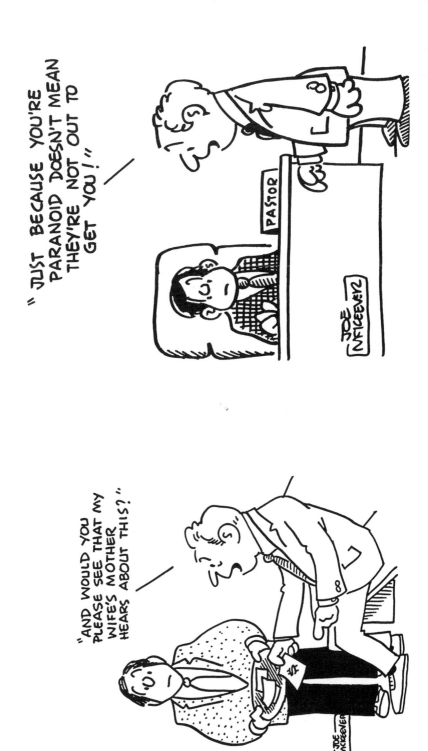

"READING FROM THE COMPUTERIZED VERSION OF THE HOLY BIBLE.... 'AND JESUS CHOSE TWELVE, THAT THEY MIGHT NETWORK WITH HIM....' "

"AND WE WISH TO THANK MY MOTHER FOR THE NEW STAINED GLASS WINDOW."

"DEACON JONES SAYS HE WANTS TO SEE THE HOSS — BE CAREFUL, PASTOR — HE'S WEARING SPURS!"

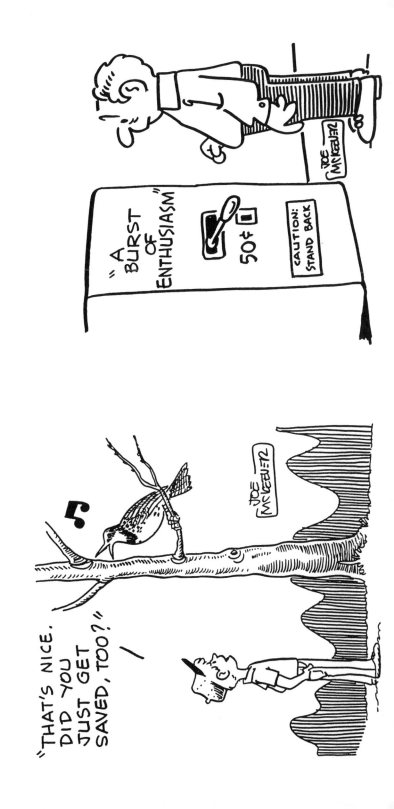

"QUICK — BEFORE ONE OF MY CHURCH MEMBERS COMES IN — DROP IN SOMETHING FOR NERVES, INDIGESTION, STRESS, AND THAT GENERAL DEAD-BATTERY FEELING."

"THE NEW PASTOR AT SALEM HAS RECEIVED NO AWARDS, HAS NO DEGREES, HAS NEVER BEEN TO THE HOLY LAND, AND IS NOT IN DEMAND FOR REVIVALS! AT LAST I'VE FOUND A PREACHER WHO CAN UNDERSTAND HOW IT FEELS TO BE ME!"